AF225407

Accounting for
Real Estate Brokerages

Steven M. Bragg

Copyright © 2025 by AccountingTools, Inc. All rights reserved.

Published by AccountingTools, Inc., Centennial, Colorado.

No part of this publication may be reproduced, stored in a retrieval system, or transmitted in any form or by any means, except as permitted under Section 107 or 108 of the 1976 United States Copyright Act, without the prior written permission of the Publisher. Requests to the Publisher for permission should be addressed to Steven M. Bragg, 6727 E. Fremont Place, Centennial, CO 80112.

Limit of Liability/Disclaimer of Warranty: While the publisher and author have used their best efforts in preparing this book, they make no representations or warranties with respect to the accuracy or completeness of the contents of this book and specifically disclaim any implied warranties of merchantability or fitness for a particular purpose. No warranty may be created or extended by written sales materials. The advice and strategies contained herein may not be suitable for your situation. You should consult with a professional where appropriate. Neither the publisher nor author shall be liable for any loss of profit or any other commercial damages, including but not limited to special, incidental, consequential, or other damages.

ISBN 978-1-64221-144-3

For more information about AccountingTools® products, visit our Web site at www.ac-countingtools.com.

Table of Contents

About the Author

Steven Bragg, CPA, has been the chief financial officer or controller of four companies, as well as a consulting manager at Ernst & Young. He received a master's degree in finance from Bentley College, an MBA from Babson College, and a Bachelor's degree in Economics from the University of Maine. He has been a two-time president of the Colorado Mountain Club, and is an avid alpine skier, mountain biker, and certified master diver. Mr. Bragg resides in Centennial, Colorado. He has written more than 300 books and courses, including *New Controller Guidebook*, *GAAP Guidebook*, and *Payroll Management*.

Steven maintains the accountingtools.com web site, which contains continuing professional education courses, the Accounting Best Practices podcast, and thousands of articles on accounting subjects.

Buy Additional AccountingTools Courses

AccountingTools offers more than 1,500 hours of CPE courses, with concentrations in accounting, auditing, finance, taxation, and ethics. Related courses that you might like include:

- Auditing Construction Contractors
- Construction Accounting
- Property Management Accounting
- Real Estate Accounting
- Real Estate Investing
- Real Estate Tax Guide

Go to accountingtools.com/cpe to view these additional courses.

Accounting for Real Estate Brokerages

Introduction

A real estate brokerage acts as an intermediary between the sellers and purchasers of real estate. It typically focuses on relatively small market areas or property types, for which it has developed a high level of expertise. It may form networks with other brokerages, in order to give its listings broader distribution. A brokerage may act as a generalist or a specialist. If it operates in a rural market, a brokerage will likely have to engage in all possible activities to remain solvent, such as selling both residential and commercial properties, brokering industrial land, and managing and appraising real estate. The path chosen usually depends on whether there is sufficient demand for niche services. For example, if there is sufficient demand for just ranches, or waterfront properties, or condominiums, then a brokerage could specialize in one of these areas.

This manual covers the accounting transactions in which a real estate brokerage engages, as well as how a brokerage presents its financial statements. The proper recordation and reporting of brokerage transactions is needed to gain a realistic understanding of its performance and financial position.

Cash Basis Accounting vs. Accrual Basis Accounting

Before delving into the many accounting issues associated with real estate brokerages, it is important to describe the cash basis of accounting and the accrual basis of accounting, since a brokerage may use one or the other to record transactions.

Under the cash basis, revenue is recorded when cash is received from clients or other brokerages, and expenses are recorded when cash is paid to suppliers and employees. It is most commonly used by smaller brokerages with less complex accounting systems. Under the accrual basis, revenue is recorded when earned and expenses are recorded when consumed. It is most commonly used by larger brokerages with more complex accounting systems. The key difference between the two methods is in the timing of transaction recordation. When aggregated over time, the results of the two methods are approximately the same. The timing difference between the methods occurs because revenue recognition is delayed under the cash basis until inbound payments arrive at the brokerage. Similarly, the recognition of expenses under the cash basis can be delayed until such time as a supplier invoice is paid. To apply these concepts, here are several examples:

- *Revenue recognition.* In June, the Jones brokerage refers a client to the Smith brokerage in exchange for a 0.5% sales commission if the referral results in a property purchase. The client does purchase a property, which closes in September, resulting in a $5,000 referral fee to be paid by the Smith brokerage in October. Under the cash basis of accounting, the Jones brokerage can record the $5,000 when the cash is received in October. Under the accrual basis, the Jones brokerage can record the $5,000 as soon as the deal closes, in September.

- *Expense recognition.* A brokerage buys $500 of office supplies in May, which it pays for in June. Under the cash basis of accounting, the brokerage recognizes the purchase in June, when it pays the bill. Under the accrual basis, the brokerage recognizes the purchase in May, when it receives the supplier's invoice.

Brokerage Revenues

The bulk of the revenue generated by a brokerage are the commissions generated from representing clients in their real estate transactions. This may involve the representation of a seller, or a purchaser, or both parties. A much smaller proportion of the firm's revenues come from referrals, derived from the referral of clients to other brokerages.

The Nature of Sales Commissions

A brokerage earns a commission based on the type of arrangement it has with a seller. For example, if the seller accepts the firm's standard listing package, then the fee may be 2.5% of the eventual sale price. The listing package may include agency representation, listing exposure, and the firm's oversight of the sale transaction through the closing. Or, the brokerage may earn a lesser commission if the seller wants to take on some of these responsibilities, such as showing their property to prospective buyers and taking on closing responsibilities. In short, the benefits provided by the brokerage should be commensurate with the commission rate charged.

Sales Commissions

The primary form of brokerage revenue is the sales commission. This is derived from a sale transaction in which a broker or agent working for the brokerage is paid either a percentage of the sale price or a fixed fee. The seller of the property pays the commission, after which the fee is split between the brokerage and the broker or agent that was responsible for the deal. In a minority of cases, the commission may be paid by a property purchaser, which hires the firm to locate property for it.

The commission rate paid by the seller is stated in the listing agreement, to which the signatories are the brokerage firm and the property owner. For example, it might state that the seller will pay a 5% commission on the sale price, where the listing brokerage and the buyer's agent equally split the proceeds.

Of the commission amount paid to the brokerage, there will then be a further split, where the firm retains a portion of the amount and the remainder is paid to the agent or broker responsible for the specific sale. This split is stated in the contract that each agent or broker signed with the brokerage when he or she joined it. For example, the agreement might state that the brokerage retains 25% of all commissions received, with the remainder being forwarded to the agent or broker.

EXAMPLE

Rachael Yusupova is an agent with the Parsons Real Estate Brokerage. When she joined the brokerage, she agreed to a 75/25 commission split arrangement with Parsons. She represents Marlene Rhoades, who has just purchased a high-end condominium for $3 million. The listing agreement states that the seller will pay a 5% commission on the final sale price, which will be split evenly between the listing firm and the buyer's representative. Based on this information, the total commission paid out will be $150,000, of which Parsons Real Estate will receive $75,000. Of that $75,000, Parsons will retain $18,750, while Rachael will receive $56,250.

The journal entries that Parsons will need to make to record this transaction are as follows:

	Debit	Credit
Cash [asset]	75,000	
Revenue – commissions [revenue]		75,000
To record commission revenue		

	Debit	Credit
Brokerage commission expense [expense]	56,250	
Cash [asset]		56,250
To record brokerage commission paid to Rachael Yusupova		

Based on these journal entries, Parsons received $75,000 and paid out $56,250 to Ms. Yusupova, resulting in a gross profit of $18,750.

In the preceding example, the commission revenue and brokerage commission expense should both be recognized within the period in which the related real estate deal closed, if the accrual basis of accounting is used. Under the cash basis, revenue is recorded when cash is received, and the commission expense is recorded when the payment is made.

Referral Fees

A brokerage firm may generate fees by referring some of its clients to other brokerage firms, usually because no one working for the firm has sufficient expertise in the requested market area. This may mean that the referring firm has no direct expertise in a different geographic region, or that its expertise is restricted to a specific type of property. The following example describes the referral issue in more detail.

EXAMPLE

The Hatfield Litton Brokerage receives a request from a client to assist it in acquiring a warehouse in the industrial sector of Denver, so that it can set up grow operations for a medical marijuana facility. Hatfield's people have no expertise in this area, but it can refer the matter to the Grow Green Brokerage, which only works in this area. The two brokerages sign a referral agreement, under which the referring entity (Hatfield) will receive a 0.5% commission on any property purchases made through Grow Green by its client.

A few months later, Grow Green locates an acceptable warehouse for the client, which pays $6 million for it. The Hatfield brokerage receives a referral fee of $30,000, which it records with the following entry:

	Debit	Credit
Cash [asset]	30,000	
Revenue – referral commission [revenue]		30,000
To record revenue from receipt of referral fee		

The referral was made by Denton Smith, one of the brokers working for Hatfield Litton. He knew a broker working at Grow Green, and set up the referral arrangement. He is entitled to a 75% commission on the referral fee, which Hatfield records with the following entry:

	Debit	Credit
Brokerage commission expense [expense]	22,500	
Cash [asset]		22,500
To record brokerage commission paid to Denton Smith		

Based on these journal entries, Hatfield received $30,000 and paid out $22,500, resulting in a gross profit of $7,500.

Leasing Commissions

A real estate brokerage may also generate commissions from lessors when it can locate lessees who enter into leasing arrangements with the lessors. If the brokerage uses the accrual basis of accounting, it can recognize the revenue associated with these transactions as soon as the related leasing deal closes, not when the tenant moves in. Under the cash basis of accounting, the revenue is recorded when the related cash is received. As of the deal closing date, the brokerage has completed its performance obligations, and so is entitled to payment from the lessor.

EXAMPLE

Brackett Corporation, which owns an office building, hires the Butler McNeil Brokerage to lease out the entire fifth floor of their building. After a month of searching, Sarah Owings, an agent working for Butler McNeil, finds a prospective tenant, which is willing to pay $150,000/month for the next five years. Ms. Owings is entitled to a 70% commission split with the brokerage, while Brackett has promised Butler McNeil $50,000 if it can obtain a tenant. The related journal entries made by Butler McNeil are as follows:

	Debit	Credit
Cash [asset]	50,000	
Revenue – leasing commission [revenue]		50,000
To record revenue from receipt of referral fee		

The brokerage then pays Ms. Owings her 70% share of the commission, as shown in the following entry:

	Debit	Credit
Brokerage commission expense [expense]	35,000	
Cash [asset]		35,000
To record brokerage commission paid to Sarah Owings		

Based on these journal entries, Butler McNeil received $50,000 and paid out $35,000, resulting in a gross profit of $15,000.

Leasing arrangements can differ from a property sale, in that the payment due to the brokerage from the lessor may not be received at once; instead, it may be paid out in installments over an extended period of time. When this is the case, the broker responsible for the deal will also be paid his or her share of the commission only after the brokerage has received the cash – which means that cash payouts may be substantially delayed.

EXAMPLE

Assume the same scenario as the immediately preceding example, except that the lessor has agreed to pay Butler McNeil $10,000 per month for the next five months, for a total of $50,000. The first of these payments starts in one month. In this case, the journal entry is as follows:

	Debit	Credit
Accounts receivable [asset]	50,000	
Revenue – leasing commission [revenue]		50,000
To record revenue from consummated leasing arrangement		

There is not yet a related payment to Sarah Owings, since Butler McNeil has not yet received any cash from the lessor. Instead, the brokerage (which uses the accrual basis of accounting) records the full amount payable in the form of an account payable, using the following entry:

	Debit	Credit
Brokerage commission expense [expense]	35,000	
Accounts payable [liability]		35,000
To record brokerage commission payable to Sarah Owings		

At this point, all revenue and expenses associated with the leasing deal have been recognized.

A month later, the first installment of $10,000 arrives from the lessor, which triggers the following two entries:

	Debit	Credit
Cash [asset]	10,000	
Accounts receivable [asset]		10,000
To record payment of account receivable from consummated leasing arrangement		

	Debit	Credit
Accounts payable [liability]	7,000	
Cash [asset]		7,000
To record partial payment of brokerage commission to Sarah Owings		

Assuming that the lessor will continue making $10,000 monthly payments for the next four months, the brokerage will continue making the same two entries in those months, until the receivable and payable are both fully paid off.

Brokerage Commissions on Development Projects

Brokerage involvement is essential to the success of large real estate construction projects. If a brokerage cannot find buyers or tenants, then a construction project may run out of cash and never be completed. Given the leverage that brokerages have over these projects, they can demand a portion of the brokerage fee from the developer, such as when a condominium purchaser makes a down payment on a yet-to-be-constructed unit. If so, the accounting for the payments differs from what we have previously described. Instead of recognizing revenue at once, the recognition must be delayed until the deal has actually closed (which may not take place for several years). In this situation, the brokerage recognizes any cash received as a liability, until the deal has closed.

EXAMPLE

The Farabell Roberts Real Estate Brokerage has been awarded an exclusive arrangement to sell every condominium in a 250-unit tower that is currently under construction. Farabell will receive a 2.5% commission on every condominium sold. The standard price for each unit is $800,000, so the brokerage will eventually receive $5,000,000 in commissions (calculated as 250 units × $800,000 × 2.5%). Under the terms of its agreement with the developer, Farabell will receive an $8,000 advance on its commission whenever a customer signs a sales contract to purchase a condominium. Farabell's brokers are paid a 75% commission. A Farabell broker convinces a customer to sign a sales contract for one condominium, which results in the following two journal entries:

	Debit	Credit
Cash [asset]	8,000	
Liability – deferred commission revenue [liability]		8,000
To record receipt of cash for advance on commission		

	Debit	Credit
Prepaid expense – deferred brokerage commission expense [asset]	6,000	
Cash [asset]		6,000
To record payment of deferred brokerage commission expense		

In the second entry, the prepaid expense is temporarily recorded as an asset, known as a prepaid expense. Up to this point, the brokerage has not recorded any revenues or expenses related to the transaction.

A year later, the condominium unit is completed, and the buyer takes possession. The developer then pays Farabell the remaining commission amounts due (which is an additional $12,000 on each unit sold, for a total of $20,000 on each sold unit). This results in the following two entries:

	Debit	Credit
Cash [asset]	12,000	
Liability – deferred commission revenue [liability]	8,000	
Revenue – deferred commission revenue [revenue]		20,000
To record receipt of cash and recognition of deferred revenue		

	Debit	Credit
Brokerage commission expense [expense]	15,000	
Cash [asset]		9,000
Prepaid expense – deferred brokerage commission expense [asset]		6,000
To record payment of commission expense and recognition of deferred expense		

In the first entry, debiting the liability – deferred commission revenue account eliminates the balance in that account, transferring it to the revenue account. In the second entry, crediting the prepaid expense – deferred brokerage commission expense account eliminates the balance in that account, transferring it to the expense account. At this point, all revenues and expenses associated with the sale of the condominium unit have been recognized.

Transaction Fees

A brokerage may also charge its clients transaction fees, which are separate from commissions and which offset a variety of administrative costs incurred by the brokerage to process sales transactions. The accountant may elect to record these fees as revenue, or to offset them against the original administrative costs. Either approach will result in the same amount of reported profit.

Brokerage Expenses

The primary expense of a brokerage is payments made to its agents and brokers. This compensation is usually mostly commission-based, though it may pay out a combination of commissions and a base salary. In addition, a brokerage will likely make a variety of expenditures as part of its operations, as discussed in the following subsections. They are listed in alphabetical order by topic.

Advertising Expenses

A brokerage or a network of brokerages to which it belongs will likely make ongoing expenditures on advertising. Doing so provides the firm with a market identity that is critical for attracting prospective clients to it. Advertising is also used to promote specific property listings, such as with signs (For Sale, Open House, and Sold), direct mail, and brochures. Also, depending on state licensing laws, a brokerage may be able to promote its listings in other states, in order to expand the exposure of its more unique properties to a broader range of purchasers. For the types of advertising in which a real estate brokerage would engage, all advertising costs should be charged to expense as incurred.

Compensation Expense

A larger brokerage may maintain a variety of staff positions, such as a general sales manager, leasing manager, information systems manager, training manager, and advertising manager. In addition, the sales staff may receive a modest level of base pay, plus commissions. Compensation payments to this group are made through the payroll system, which may be calculated either onsite through payroll software, or through a third-party payroll supplier. In either case, the result is a payroll register, which is a listing of what employees will be paid, along with the associated deductions from their pay.

The primary journal entry for payroll is the summary-level entry that is compiled from the payroll register. This entry usually includes debits for wages and the company's portion of payroll taxes. There will also be credits to a number of other accounts, each one detailing the liability for payroll taxes that have not been paid, as well as for the amount of cash already paid to employees for their net pay. The basic payroll journal entry is as follows:

	Debit	Credit
Compensation expense [expense]	xxx	
Payroll taxes expense [expense]	xxx	
Cash [asset]		xxx
Federal withholding taxes payable [liability]		xxx
Social security taxes payable [liability]		xxx
Medicare taxes payable [liability]		xxx
Federal unemployment taxes payable [liability]		xxx
State unemployment taxes payable [liability]		xxx
Garnishments payable [liability]		xxx

Note: The reason for the payroll taxes expense line item in this journal entry is that the company incurs the cost of matching the social security and Medicare amounts paid by employees, and directly incurs the cost of unemployment insurance. The employee-paid portions of the social security and Medicare taxes are not recorded as expenses; instead, they are liabilities for which the brokerage has an obligation to remit cash to the taxing government entity.

A key point with this journal entry is that the compensation expense contains employee gross pay, while the amount actually paid to employees through the cash account is their net pay. The difference between the two figures (which can be substantial) is the deductions from their pay, such as payroll taxes and withholdings to pay for benefits.

There may be a number of additional employee deductions to include in this journal entry. For example, there may be deductions for pension plans, health insurance, life insurance, vision insurance, and for the repayment of advances.

When withheld taxes and the brokerage's portion of payroll taxes are paid at a later date, use the following entry to reduce the balance in the cash account, and eliminate the balances in the liability accounts:

	Debit	Credit
Federal withholding taxes payable [liability]	xxx	
Social security taxes payable [liability]	xxx	
Medicare taxes payable [liability]	xxx	
Federal unemployment taxes payable [liability]	xxx	
State withholding taxes payable [liability]	xxx	
State unemployment taxes payable [liability]	xxx	
Garnishments payable [liability]	xxx	
Cash [asset]		xxx

Thus, when a brokerage initially deducts taxes and other items from an employee's pay, the brokerage incurs a liability to pay the taxes to a third party. This liability only disappears from the brokerage's accounting records when it pays the related funds to the entity to which they are owed.

If the brokerage is using the accrual basis of accounting, it should accrue an expense for a commission in the same period when the accountant records the sale generated by an agent or broker, *and* when it can calculate the amount of the commission. This is a debit to the commission expense account and a credit to a commission liability account.

EXAMPLE

Wes Smith earns a $15,000 commission on a property sale, and will be paid on the 15th day of the following month. At the end of the accounting period in which Mr. Smith generates the sale, his brokerage (which uses the accrual basis of accounting) creates the following entry to record its liability for the commission:

	Debit	Credit
Commission expense [expense]	15,000	
Accrued commissions [liability]		15,000
To record the initial liability to pay a commission		

The brokerage then reverses the entry at the beginning of the following accounting period, because it is going to record the actual payment on the 15th of the month. Thus, the reversing entry is:

	Debit	Credit
Accrued commissions [liability]	15,000	
Commission expense [expense]		15,000
To reverse prior month's commission accrual		

On the 15th of the month, the brokerage pays Mr. Smith his commission and records this entry:

	Debit	Credit
Commission expense [expense]	15,000	
Cash [asset]		15,000
To record the payment of a commission		

For a more substantial discussion of payroll accounting, see the author's *Payroll Management* book.

Costs to Fulfill a Contract

In general, any costs required to fulfill a contract should be recognized as assets, as long as they meet all of these criteria:

- The costs are tied to a specific contract;
- The costs will be used to satisfy future performance obligations; and
- There is an expectation that the costs will be recovered.

Costs that are considered to relate directly to a contract include the following:

- *Direct labor.* Includes the wages of those employees directly engaged in providing services to the client.
- *Direct materials.* Includes the supplies consumed in the provision of services to the client.
- *Cost allocations.* Includes those costs that relate directly to the contract, such as the cost of managing the contract, project supervision, and depreciation of the equipment used to fulfill the contract.
- *Chargeable costs.* Includes those costs that the contract explicitly states can be charged to the client.
- *Other costs.* Includes costs that would only be incurred because the brokerage entered into the contract, such as payments to subcontractors providing services to the client.

Other costs are to be charged to expense as incurred, rather than being classified as contract assets. These costs include:

- *Administration*. General and administrative costs, unless the contract terms explicitly state that they can be charged to the contract.
- *Indistinguishable*. Costs for which it is not possible to determine whether they relate to unsatisfied or satisfied performance obligations. In this case, the default assumption is that they relate to satisfied performance obligations.
- *Past performance costs*. Any costs incurred that relate to performance obligations that have already been fulfilled.
- *Waste*. The costs of resources wasted in the contract fulfillment process, which were not included in the contract price.

EXAMPLE

The Throckmorton Brokerage enters into a contract to run a call center that sells timeshares, where the other party is a business that owns the timeshares. Throckmorton incurs a cost of $150,000 to construct a call management system for the call center. This cost relates to activities needed to fulfill the requirements of the contract. This cost should be amortized over the term of the contract.

When contract-related costs have been recognized as assets, they should be amortized on a systematic basis that reflects the timing of the transfer of related services to the client. If there is a change in the anticipated timing of the transfer of goods and services to the client, update the amortization to reflect this change.

Costs to Obtain a Contract

It is acceptable for a brokerage to capitalize the costs incurred to obtain a contract, though only if there is a reasonable expectation that those costs will be recovered. The costs that can be capitalized in this manner are essentially any that the brokerage would not have incurred if it had not obtained the contract. This concept can be flipped around to apply to a lessor, as noted in the following example.

EXAMPLE

Eskimo Construction builds an office tower, which it expects to lease out to various medical providers. It contracts with Sunshine Real Estate Brokers to find medical establishments willing to lease space in the office tower. As a result, Eskimo pays Sunshine a total of $620,000. This represents a cost of obtaining a lease agreement with each tenant, so Eskimo can amortize the $620,000 over the lives of the various lease agreements that Sunshine obtained.

Any costs incurred by the brokerage to obtain a contract that would have been incurred even in the absence of the contract should be charged to expense in the period incurred; they are not capitalized. The only exception is when these costs can be charged to the customer even if the contract is not obtained.

Equipment and Supplies

A brokerage will pay modest amounts for toner cartridges, office supplies, postage, paper, and kitchen and restroom supplies. Though some of these items may not be used at once, they are always charged to expense as incurred; the amounts involved are too immaterial to be worth capitalizing and charging to expense over a few additional months as they are actually used.

Franchise Fees

If a brokerage has entered into a franchise agreement with a national franchisor, then it is gaining the name recognition that comes with the marketing efforts of the franchisor. In this case, the brokerage will be required to pay a portion of its revenue to the franchisor as a royalty, as well as entry and exit fees, and referral fees. The franchisor may mandate other expenditures, such as for signage or local advertising.

When a brokerage franchisee pays an initial franchise fee to a franchisor, this payment can be considered an intangible asset. It is permissible for the brokerage to recognize this cost as an asset, since it is an asset acquired from a third party. The franchisee should amortize this asset over its estimated useful life, which is presumed to be the term of the franchise agreement.

EXAMPLE

The Smith Dodson Real Estate Brokerage enters into a franchise arrangement with a major national brokerage franchisor, paying an up-front fee of $50,000. Smith records the payment as follows:

	Debit	Credit
Franchise fee [asset]	50,000	
Cash [asset]		50,000
To record payment of initial franchise fee		

The franchise agreement has a term of 10 years, so Smith amortizes the fee over 10 years on a straight-line basis. The first-year entry to record this amortization is:

	Debit	Credit
Amortization expense [expense]	5,000	
Accumulated amortization [contra asset]		5,000
To record annual amortization of franchise fee		

This intangible asset should be tested for impairment at least annually. If the carrying amount of the asset exceeds its fair value, write the remaining balance down to its fair value. In the assessment of impairment, review all events and circumstances that could affect the determination of fair value, such as:

- Increases in costs that could negatively impact earnings and cash flows
- Declines in actual or planned revenue
- Regulatory, legal, contractual and other factors that limit fair value
- Litigation
- Management changes or the loss of key personnel
- Decline in the business environment or general economic conditions

---

EXAMPLE

After three years, The Smith Dodson Real Estate Brokerage has still not built the office that it is entitled to construct under its franchise agreement with the franchisor, due to the intractability of the local zoning board in granting a zoning waiver to Smith Dodson. Management concludes that there is no reasonable probability of ever being able to do so, resulting in the write-off of the remaining $35,000 of the franchise fee asset. The related journal entry is:

	Debit	Credit
Impairment loss [expense]	35,000	
Accumulated impairment losses [contra asset]		35,000
To record impairment of the remaining franchise fee asset		

Smith's accountant then removes the franchise fee asset from the firm's accounting records with the following entry:

	Debit	Credit
Accumulated impairment losses [contra asset]	35,000	
Accumulated amortization [contra asset]	15,000	
Franchise fee [asset]		50,000
To remove franchise fee from the accounting records		

A franchisee may be required to pay a renewal fee to extend the term of the original franchise agreement. The accounting for this fee is the same as was used for the initial franchise fee.

Depending on the arrangement with its agents and brokers, a brokerage can mandate that they pay for a portion of the ongoing costs of affiliation with the franchisor.

Insurance Expenses

A brokerage may pay for liability, errors and omissions, and property insurance, as well as medical insurance for its employees. In all cases, it is common for the insurer to bill for the insurance in advance of the coverage period. If the brokerage pays the insurer before the coverage period begins, then (if it is using the accrual basis of accounting) the payment should be recorded as a prepaid expense (which is an asset); the prepaid expense is then converted into an expense during the coverage period. Or, if the firm is using the cash basis of accounting, then it should record the payment as an expense as soon as the payment is made.

EXAMPLE

The Burton Real Estate Brokerage purchases a bundle of insurance products from a local insurance agent for $24,000, with the coverage lasting for the next 12 months. Burton uses the accrual basis of accounting, so it uses the following entry to initially record the payment within the prepaid expenses (asset) account:

	Debit	Credit
Prepaid expenses [asset]	24,000	
Cash [asset]		24,000
To record payment for insurance products as a prepaid expense		

In each of the following months, the brokerage records the following entry to charge 1/12th of the asset to expense:

	Debit	Credit
Insurance expense [expense]	2,000	
Prepaid expenses [asset]		2,000
To charge a portion of prepaid insurance asset to expense		

Maintenance and Cleaning Expenses

The typical brokerage office will periodically experience maintenance issues, such as plumbing, electrical, or carpentry fixes. In addition, it will need to pay for ongoing cleaning activities. In both cases, the related expenditures should be charged to expense as incurred. However, if a maintenance expenditure results in an asset having a longer useful life or upgraded capabilities (such as extensive roof repairs), this expenditure can be classified as a fixed asset and depreciated over time.

Multiple Listing Service Fees

A multiple listing service (MLS) is a database established by cooperating real estate brokers to provide data about properties for sale. An MLS allows brokers to see one another's listings of properties for sale, with the goal of connecting sellers and purchasers. An MLS also provides its subscribing members with competitive market analysis data, sample contracts, and worksheets for estimating ownership and closing costs.

Brokerages pay dues or a membership fee for access to each MLS they use. These fees are typically charged to expense as incurred.

Property Maintenance

In some cases, a brokerage may become more deeply involved in the maintenance of a listed property. For example, the seller may have taken a job elsewhere and needs to have the brokerage supervise painting the exterior, mowing the lawn, or winterizing the property to prevent plumbing damage. The firm may decide to hire a property maintenance director who oversees the work of contractors in dealing with these issues. In these cases, the costs are separately accumulated against the relevant property, and then deducted from the sale price when the property is eventually sold.

Rent Expense

The owners of a brokerage may feel that having an office positioned in a prime location is critical to bringing in more buyer foot traffic. If so, rent expense will be a significantly greater proportion of total expenses than if the office were situated in a low-rent district. A variation on the concept is the virtual office, where a much smaller office is maintained that provides reception courtesies and business space, but nothing else. All other staff time is spent working from home. This latter approach greatly reduces the rent expense. For accrual basis accounting, rent payments are charged to expense in the related period of property usage. For cash basis accounting, rent payments are charged to expense when paid.

Shared Space and Services

Some brokerages may band together and operate under the same roof, where they share conference rooms, other common spaces, and administrative staff. In this situation, one of the brokerage entities typically takes responsibility for paying those bills that will be shared among the brokerages, and then bills the other brokerages for their share of the expenses.

EXAMPLE

The Anderson Morgan Real Estate Brokerage shares facilities with three other brokerages, and acts as the principal for billing purposes. In the most recent month, Anderson paid out $35,000 for the building rent, utilities, cleaning, and maintenance charges. These bills are split evenly among the four brokerages, each of which occupies the same square footage within the building. Anderson's accountant initially charges the entire amount to the firm's occupancy expense account with the following entry:

	Debit	Credit
Occupancy expense [expense]	35,000	
Cash [asset]		35,000
To record building occupancy charges to expense		

The accountant then rebills 75% of this expense to the other brokerages, using the following entry:

	Debit	Credit
Accounts receivable [asset]	26,250	
Occupancy expense [expense]		26,250
To record rebilling of occupancy expenses to co-tenants		

The other tenants then pay the billed amounts back to Anderson, resulting in the following entry:

	Debit	Credit
Cash [asset]	26,250	
Accounts receivable [asset]		26,250
To record payment of rebilled occupancy expenses		

These transactions result in a net occupancy expense for the Anderson brokerage of $8,750.

Utilities Expense

This classification includes the costs of electricity, heating, Internet, and phone fees. These costs are charged to expense as incurred.

Virtual Office Expenses

If the brokerage staff mostly works from home, then other support expenses will be incurred, such as Internet fees, an answering service, cell phone charges, and virtual assistant[1] fees. These costs are charged to expense as incurred.

---

[1] A virtual assistant is an independent contractor who provides administrative services to clients while operating outside of the client's office. This person typically operates from a home office but can access the necessary planning documents, such as a shared calendar, remotely.

Brokerage Assets

A brokerage will expend funds for a certain number of assets. It is likely to pay for leasehold improvements, if it has entered into a property lease. Leasehold improvements are defined as the enhancements paid for by a tenant to leased space. These improvements are likely to include partitions, paneling, lighting, walls, ceilings, restrooms, a kitchen, heating and air conditioning, Internet and telecommunications cabling, carpeting, and window blinds and drapes.

When a brokerage pays for leasehold improvements, they should be recorded as a fixed asset and then amortized over the shorter of their useful life or the remaining term of the lease. For amortization purposes, the remaining term of the lease can be extended into additional lease renewal periods if the renewal is reasonably assured (such as when there is a bargain renewal option).

> **Note:** Technically, the brokerage is amortizing leasehold improvements rather than depreciating them. The reason is that the landlord owns the improvements, so the brokerage is only exercising an intangible right to use the improvements during the term of the lease – and intangible assets are amortized, not depreciated.

EXAMPLE

The Steiner Real Estate Brokerage has a five-year lease on office space, as well as an option to renew the lease for an additional five years at the then-prevailing market rate. Steiner pays $150,000 to build offices in its leased space immediately after it leases the space. The useful life of these offices is 20 years. Since there is no bargain purchase option to renew the lease, it is not reasonably assured that Steiner will renew the lease. Consequently, it should amortize the $150,000 over the five years of the existing lease, which is the shorter of the useful life of the improvements or the lease term. Steiner will recognize the amortization in each of the five years of the lease with the following entry:

	Debit	Credit
Amortization expense [expense]	30,000	
Accumulated amortization [contra asset]		30,000
To record annual amortization on leasehold improvements		

A brokerage will also need to furnish its premises, which typically involves the purchase of desks, chairs, credenzas, filing cabinets, reception accommodations, and so forth. These purchases are usually recorded within the furniture and fixtures asset account. A common depreciation period for this asset classification is seven years.

A brokerage cannot realistically exist without computers for every employee. These assets are usually capitalized, rather than being charged to expense, which means that they are recorded as fixed assets. Desktop computers should be depreciated over a period of anywhere from three to five years, depending on the firm's history regarding how frequently they need to be replaced. Laptop and tablet computers usually receive much rougher treatment and so are replaced more frequently – usually resulting in a useful life of just two or three years for depreciation purposes.

A brokerage will also need sales management software, which is used to monitor transaction activity, pending closings, and listings about to expire, as well as tracking business by office and salesperson. This software may be purchased and stored locally, or accessed as a subscription service.

EXAMPLE

The Okamoto Brokerage has just spent $12,000 to acquire five laptop computers for its sales staff. The laptops will be used hard, and so are only expected to last for two years, after which they will be replaced. The firm's standard practice is to give the old laptops to their sales staff for personal use after two years, which is a good way to encourage them not to break the computers. Based on this information, the brokerage initially records the purchase with the following entry:

	Debit	Credit
Fixed assets – computers [asset]	12,000	
Cash [asset]		12,000
To record the purchase of five laptop computers		

In each of the following months, the brokerage records the following depreciation entry, which charges the laptops to expense over 24 months:

	Debit	Credit
Depreciation expense [expense]	500	
Accumulated depreciation [contra asset]		500
To record monthly depreciation expense on five purchased laptop computers		

The accumulated depreciation resulting from the preceding entry is paired with and offsets the fixed assets line item in the brokerage's balance sheet.

Real Estate Brokerage Reporting

A real estate brokerage reports its financial results and financial position, respectively, in an income statement and balance sheet. Both reports are described in the following sub-sections.

The Income Statement

The income statement shows all revenues and expenses incurred during a reporting period (such as a month, quarter, or year), resulting in a profit or loss. A sample format for a real estate brokerage's income statement appears in the following exhibit.

Farabell Roberts Real Estate Brokerage
Income Statement
For the Month Ended January 31, 20X1

Gross Sales		
Sales commissions	$ ______	
Leasing commissions	$ ______	
Referral fees	$ ______	
Total gross sales		$ ______
Operating Expenses		
Salesperson commissions	$ ______	
Referral fees	$ ______	
MLS fees	$ ______	
Franchise fees	$ ______	
Other operating expenses	$ ______	
Total cost of sales		$ ______
Advertising expense	$ ______	
Compensation expense	$ ______	
Benefit expense	$ ______	
Rent expense	$ ______	
Equipment and supplies expense	$ ______	
Maintenance and cleaning expense	$ ______	
Dues and subscription expense	$ ______	
Accounting, legal, and consulting expense	$ ______	
Insurance expense	$ ______	
Taxes and licenses expense	$ ______	
Travel and entertainment expense	$ ______	
Utilities expense	$ ______	
Total operating expenses		$ ______
Net income (loss)		$ ______

A brokerage may be organized into a group of profit centers, where the revenues and expenses of each cluster of sales and support staff are tracked and reported separately – usually on a trend line. This approach is highly recommended, because it allows for the identification of work groups that are not generating a profit, or a sub-standard one.

The Balance Sheet

A balance sheet lays out the ending balances in a brokerage's asset, liability, and equity accounts as of the date stated on the report. As such, it provides a picture of what the firm owns and owes, as well as how much has been invested in it. The information listed on the balance sheet must comply with the formula below, which states that the aggregate amount of all assets on the balance sheet must equal the total of all liabilities and equity on the report, which is known as the accounting equation.

$$\text{Total assets} = \text{Total liabilities} + \text{Equity}$$

A sample format for a real estate brokerage's balance sheet appears in the following exhibit.

Farabell Roberts Real Estate Brokerage
Balance Sheet
As of January 31, 20X1

Assets

Cash and cash equivalents	$	
Accounts receivable	$	
Investments	$	
Fixed assets	$	
Less: Accumulated depreciation and amortization	$	
Other assets	$	
Total assets		$

Liabilities

Accounts payable	$	
Taxes payable	$	
Current portion of long-term debt	$	
Long-term debt	$	
Other non-current liabilities	$	
Total liabilities		$

Equity

Capital stock	$	
Retained earnings	$	
Total equity		$
Total liabilities and equity		$

Summary

There are several areas in which the accounting for real estate brokerages varies from that of other businesses. First, the bulk of its revenue comes from commissions, for which there are several variations. Also, a brokerage incurs several unique expenses, including multiple listing service fees, virtual office expenses, and franchise fees. It may also have to initially record some contract-related costs as assets, and later charge them to expense. The result is a unique blend of issues for the accountant to deal with.

Glossary

A

Accrual basis of accounting. When revenue is recorded when earned and expenses are recorded when consumed.

Amortization. The process of incrementally charging the cost of an intangible asset to expense over its expected period of use.

B

Balance sheet. A report that lays out the ending balances in a brokerage's asset, liability, and equity accounts as of the date stated on the report.

C

Cash basis accounting. When revenue is recorded as cash is received from clients or other brokerages, and expenses are recorded as cash is paid to suppliers and employees.

Commission. A fee paid for services in facilitating a sale transaction.

D

Depreciation. The process of incrementally charging the cost of a tangible asset to expense over its expected period of use.

F

Franchise. The right granted to a business to market another entity's services in a particular territory.

I

Income statement. A report that shows all revenues and expenses incurred during a reporting period, resulting in a profit or loss.

M

Multiple listing service. A database established by cooperating real estate brokers to provide data about properties for sale.

P

Payroll register. A listing of what employees will be paid, along with the associated deductions from their pay.

Index

www.ingramcontent.com/pod-product-compliance
Lightning Source LLC
Chambersburg PA
CBHW080320030726
47593CB00009B/2823